Angelic Sigil

142 Ways to Make Instant Contact with Angels and Archangels

Ben Woodcroft

Table of Contents

The Keys to Angelic Contact

You could look to heaven and call out, 'In the name of God, hear me great angel Gabriel.' That might be enough to get help, if you are sincere. Or you can use the secret sigils, keys and calls that open up instant contact with the angels.

If you wish to find a thorough and effective process for contacting angels, it is divulged within these pages, but this is not a book of evocation, in that you are not calling the angels to appear before you visibly. Such ritual practice does exist, but it is complicated and, for your purposes, unnecessary. This is a book where you petition the angel to help your needs be met. In this book, there are one hundred and forty-two angels and archangels that will hear your call.

What I have set out in this book is a ritual method that is refined and advanced, while remaining simple enough for beginners. It is based on centuries of magickal knowledge, updated by several decades of research and experiment. The ritual practice has been augmented and simplified so that when you call to the angels, they hear you instantly. You will work without the wands, circles and oils of elaborate ceremonial magick, but you will be required to work with integrity and sincerity. Do this, and results will be yours.

It is your divine right to contact angels, and the exact method for doing so is set out in detail. You will be able to contact the following angels.

The Eight Angels of Virtue bring clarity, honesty and peace.

The Nine Angels of Thrones work primarily with the emotions.

The Eleven Archangels bring help when you are faced with major life changes.

The Angels of The 72 Letter Name are willing to help on many practical issues, from dealing with enemies to finding love.

The Angels of The 42 Letter Name are concerned with self-discovery and emotion.

There are one hundred and twenty-seven sigils in this book. For the Eight Angels of Virtue there is a single sigil used to contact them all. The same is true for The Nine Angels of Thrones; one sigil works for all nine. For every other angel and archangel, an individual sigil is provided. The keys that enable this magick come in the form of Admitting Words, and in some rituals, you are given specific calls.

Sigils, keys and calls are not a guarantee of contact. They are images and sounds that are used as a doorway. You must knock on the door, be heard, be invited inside, and then you must step through. That is what this magick will do for you, if you are willing to take that step through. The key to this is sincerity of need. When you have a real need, and wish for the help of the angels (rather than to order them to do as you wish), the angels are compelled to heed you, and to respond. It is true, as implied by the title of this book, that you can and will make instant contact with angels. If you follow the instructions and speak with sincerity, the contact is real and immediate, whether you feel it or not.

You will only get out of this book what you put in. If you are slothful, overly casual, filled with skepticism or cynicism, then you cannot expect the heavenly hosts to reward you with splendor. If you are open to the reality of angels and approach them with genuine expectation, you will be rewarded with powerful results in the real world.

I imagine that if you have purchased this book it is not out of academic interest, but because you seek the help of angels. If you are willing to follow the instructions, you will learn much about magick by working with the angels. I highly recommend this journey, but only if it is one that feels right for you. It is natural to be mildly skeptical, and you would be wise to wonder how I came about such knowledge. A full explanation would require an autobiography, but it's fair to say that I have been involved with modern occultism for over thirty years.

In recent months, I was reminded that the academic

authors, Skinner and Rankine, voiced concerns back in 2006 that their excellent explorations of ancient occult texts would one day be watered down and made into gruel by other authors. What they perhaps failed to notice is that since the early 1880s, and even before to some degree, occultists have been working with and adapting these materials. This is nothing new. Hidden, but not new.

Occultism is alive and growing, and occultists have been working with angelic material in many ways for longer than we have been alive. What has remained hidden from the public, and from many academics, is the extent to which workable angelic magick has been simplified and continues to be practiced today.

By the early 1980s, primary source materials had been developed into new, workable sigils and rituals, arguably more powerful than the blurred, misspelled and error-filled documents of old.

What you find in this book are sigils, keys and calls that are based on the best sources, but further advanced by working occultists who were driven to develop them through their genuine need. Driven by need, occultists moved beyond the confines of theory and tradition, finding ways to make magick more potent than the scholarly rituals of convention.

Some of this new material has been revealed by other authors in recent years, in other forms, and it is expected that this process will continue.

I mention Skinner and Rankine, and their work, not to criticize, but to provide you with some context. If this book appears to be a collection of invented ideas and fictional angelic names, you would be wise to do some research. But heed this warning: you may not find what you want on the world-wide-web. Respected authors, while not providing practical material most of the time, *will* guide you more effectively than the internet.

I have taken on many students of magick and have found that a little knowledge can be a dangerous thing, and that a miasma of information leads to blurred thinking. That is, when given secret magickal information, a student may be tempted to the world of Google, to find out everything about a given angel. The internet does not know everything, and the better secrets are hidden. If you search for the angel names in this book, many of them are not listed online, or even in reputable angel dictionaries, or the encyclopedias sold by the major occult publishers.

You will find these angels named in books such as *The Sixth and Seventh Books of Moses* (sometimes hidden in footnotes), and you will find them throughout the history of occult literature. The word you should note is *occult*. It means *hidden*. Despite a mass of occult 'information' that exists online, many of these names remain hidden. Many are known, but much remains concealed from the ordinary world. It is concealed in many ways, but often, quite simply, in books. This matters because for every website trying to peddle useful information, there are ten uninformed bloggers that will try to convince you that every angel is actually a demon. If you trust the internet, you will never perform any magick, but if you seek out practical books and explore the occult for yourself, you will find truth.

I do not ask you to trust me, but say that if you do not trust the work in this book, then you should do thorough research of your own. You should then consult working and knowledgeable occultists, and read my blog posts to form an opinion about me. In general, the internet is almost guaranteed to frighten you with lies and, more often, gradual distortions of the truth that occur when information is spread and copied, copied and spread, from site to site, with the remains barely even chiming with the reality of angelic magick.

This is why I can say with great confidence, that the magick described here will work, even though there are many who will tell you that it cannot work unless you follow the old rules. What I share in this book is what I've found to be a balance between simplicity and effect.

During these rituals, you need to say the angelic names, along with divine names and other holy words of power. At the end of the book, there's an explanation of what these words all mean, so you know what it is you're saying. This information is optional. If you don't want to know the meaning of the words, that is fine, because they work.

Your pronunciation does not have to be perfect, because there is no single way to pronounce these words and names, just as there is no single way to pronounce your name. Everybody says these names differently. But to make it easy the important names are also spelled out phonetically. A word like Adonai, will also be shown as ADD-OH-NIGH. The words in capitals are very easy to pronounce. Put it together and you get the right sound. If you're still concerned, or want to learn faster, I've made it even easier by putting videos on the website (www.thepowerofmagick.com) with all the pronunciations you need. Everything reads as though it's in English, but note that the G sound is always like the G in grow or give, *not* the sound you get from germ or gender.

I have found that writing out the ritual, before you begin, is a worthwhile aspect of the ritual. Writing it out by hand (not typing it up on a computer), may take a few minutes, but can be a settling and focusing experience that helps prepare you for the magick. This also gives you the option to write it out phonetically, which can make the ritual easier to follow. If you are using the eBook this will help you keep the required sigil in view, without having to move back and forth through the book. Even if you are using the print version of the book, you should consider this a worthwhile exercise.

With so many angels and powers to choose from, it can be difficult to know where to start. I strongly suggest that you find the time to read the whole book before you work any magick. Become familiar with the different angels and how they can help. One reading of this book should give you enough insight into the angels to know which might be relevant for you. Do not always go to the archangels, seeking the greatest power. True power comes from relevance and sincerity, so take the time to choose your angel carefully, and then work the magick with confidence.

The Preparatory Working

Employ this working at the beginning of every angelic ritual in the book. To prepare, make this time feel special and set aside from ordinary life. Your ritual should not feel like something you fit in between dinner and an evening of TV. You may actually perform your ritual between dinner and an evening of TV, and that is acceptable, but the time should feel special. Your ritual will call to the messengers of God, and although the magick has been simplified, it must be sincere.

The ritual may only take you ten or fifteen minutes, but it should feel sincere, as though you are genuinely trying to contact angels to solve a problem. You are not saying a spell and hoping for change, but actually contacting angels and communicating your need.

Think of it this way; if an angel appeared before you, in all its bright glory, how would you react? How would you act? You would not rush through your ritual in a casual and distracted manner. You would be made humble by awe. Consider this, and know that you should assume this attitude in every ritual. Be humble and awed, as though the angel is there, because if you believe in this magick then you know that the angel *is* there. You are not calling it to appear visibly (though some angels may disclose their presence through a sound, a fragrance, a glimpse of flickering light), but the angel is present whether you sense anything or not. You are using divine names to call a messenger of God to help create the change that you desire. Simple as the magick may be, it cannot be anything other than sacred to you.

I like to work at night, after dark, in a low-lit room, often illuminated only by a single candle. It can also be pleasant to work outdoors, if you are fortunate enough to have a private space that allows this. You may prefer to work at dawn. If you can only perform that ritual in fifteen stolen minutes, while everybody is out of the house, that is also going to work, but try to make it feel special and sacred, and remember the enormity of what you are attempting.

When you have found a time and place to perform the ritual without disturbance or distraction, you may sit, kneel, stand or even lie down, but for the sake of practicality, put yourself in a comfortable place where this book (or your notebook), is clearly visible and readily to hand.

Chant EE-AH-OH-EH three times.

This sound, EE-AH-OH-EH, is a vocalization of the name of God, known as the Tetragrammaton, and is often written in English as YHWH, and sometimes spoken as Yahweh. It can even be vocalized by naming the Hebrew letters, as something like YORD HEY VARV HEY – there are many variations on this, some accurate and some not so accurate.

I have found that when you run the sounds of EE, AH, OH and EH together, it sounds similar to Yahweh, but not quite the same. In this book, YHWH is pronounced as EE-AH-OH-EH. This sound is also quite close to the Greek IAO (pronounced EE-AH-OH, which is a name of God that is used in many magickal traditions.)

I believe that it helps to think of these short sounds as resonances that lead to the name of God. This is more useful than thinking that God's name is actually Yahweh. There are many names of God, so consider these as a pathway to God, however you perceive God.

Chant those sounds three times, and as you do so know that you are calling on creation itself. That is, you are calling to be an active part of creation, to work with God, to let God work through you. Your choices, decisions and desires are all in place, they are allowed; that is free will. But you are calling on God to give you the authority to speak to angels. These feelings, although brief, are important, so allow yourself to feel that as the ritual begins you are actively taking part in the conscious creation of your future. You are not merely reacting to life, but taking charge of the future, and you are doing so with the power of creation that has been bestowed upon you. While it could be said that angels are hidden, secret and difficult to contact, at this moment you should know that it is your divine right to speak to angels, and to ask that they respond to your wishes. Take a few moments to let yourself feel the absolute 'rightness' of this situation and of your magickal work.

In many of the source materials that led to this work, confession plays a major role, with extensive cleansing and a considerable number of requests for forgiveness, as well as many statements about your own lack of worth. In the centuries that followed, much of this material was dropped from ritual practice, as it was suspected it had been included only to appease those who might otherwise find the magick to be sacrilegious. In more recent times, however, it has been found that a variation on this feeling can be useful. As you begin the ritual, you can observe your feeling of regret about the situation you want to change.

I am not suggesting that you let yourself become filled with guilt and misery, as that serves no purpose. The magickal space should be a positive place. This is more akin to the feeling you get when you visit a counselor or psychologist. You discuss your problems or feelings, and then you feel less guilty. You feel better, more hopeful.

In this ritual, I do not suggest confessing your sins to God. If that's something you wish to do, it can be done at another time. Within the ritual, you should merely consider the situation, and look at all you have done to shape this situation, and let your feelings arise. Let us imagine, for a moment, that you a performing a ritual to ease an ongoing sickness (and you are calling on the angel Lelahel to assist with this). Spend a few moments thinking about how the sickness arose. Whether it arose through pure bad luck, or through your neglect, is not relevant. What you want to think about is how you felt before the sickness began, how you felt as it developed. You then consider how you tried to solve the problem, and how the feeling of being beaten by the sickness built. Think about how those feelings built until now, at this point, you have turned to magick.

This is not a confession. You are not saying sorry for becoming ill. What you are doing (and what may have been secretly implied in some of those ancient rituals) is you are observing your life as it was before the problem, and observing the way it affected you, and recognizing where you are right now. You are feeling everything that led you to work this magick. This will be repeated with a variation later in the ritual, so it is important.

Again, chant EE-AH-OH-EH three times. With the first chant, allow yourself to feel hope that your problem will be solved. With the second, feel certain that the angels will hear you. With the final chant, change this feeling to one of calm acceptance, because you know that the angel will help you. These brief chants require an act of wilful imagination. You do not need to picture anything, but you should let yourself feel hope, certainty and calm acceptance of change.

All you have done is sit down, said EE-AH-OH-EH, and then had some thoughts and feelings, and then repeated the chant. It sounds like very little, but this is the opening of the ritual and you are doing magick. Do not neglect this opening section of the ritual. I will summarise the opening process, but do not use this summary until you understand the deeper meaning of what has already been written.

Find a time and place to work your magick in peace.

Chant EE-AH-OH-EH three times. As you do, know that you are calling to be an active part of creation and that your free will gives you the authority to call angels.

In silence, take a few moments to know that it is your divine right to ask the angels to respond to your call.

In silence, think about the situation you wish to change with magick. Think about how you felt before

it arose. Think about how you felt as the situation became worse, and all that you did to right the situation. Acknowledge the feelings that brought you to this moment of need.

Chant EE-AH-OH-EH three times, and allow yourself to feel hope that your problem will be solved, certainty that the angel will hear you, and calm acceptance of the fact that the angel will help you.

The Central Working

The central working is essentially the same for every angel in this book, but there are a few minor differences. In this chapter I will use the example of the archangel Metatron, but you should know that for each class of angels, the main ritual is slightly different. The purpose of this chapter is to show you the overall ritual structure, and how you are meant to think and feel at each stage of the ritual. The exact ritual wording you need for each class of angels will be provided at the relevant part of the book.

You have performed The Preparatory Ritual, and you now look at the angel's sigil and say the angel's name out loud, three times. In this case, it would be: Metatron, Metatron, Metatron. When you look at the sigil, you do not have to study it, but you should know and believe that the sigil is an embodiment of the angel. It's like looking at a photograph of your father. The photograph is merely a blend of colors and shades, but to you it is a reminder of your father, a gateway to your memories and an understanding of who your father is to you. When you look at the sigil, you should know that it is like a reminder of the angel (even if you've never met this angel before). It is a gateway to the angel. By having the sigil with you, and seeing it as you call the angel's name three times, you experience a powerful moment of magick.

Make sure you feel as though you are actually calling to a real entity. The following concept is not original (I have seen it in many books over many decades), but it is useful. Imagine you are calling to somebody in the next room. This is quite a different feeling to just saying that person's name out loud, because you are reaching to that person, you know they are there, out of sight but able to hear you. This is how it should feel when you look at the sigil and say the angel's name. You are calling to the angel, and asking to be heard.

What follows is the main Ritual Call, and within it there

are many names that may be familiar to you, or completely strange. By way of explanation you may wish to know what it is that you are saying and calling. Please see the later chapter of the book called *The Meaning of Names*, which explains what all the words from this Ritual Call mean.

Make the following Ritual Call, out loud:

In the Names of
El, Elohim, Adonai, Adiriron
Ehyeh-asher-Ehyeh, El Shadai,
and by the Power of Dynamis,
I call on thee, Metatron.
I call thee, Metatron, by the power of
Akatriel YHWH Tzvaot.
Hear my call, Metatron and know
that I ask…

Here you state your request, plainly and with sincerity. Do not endeavor to justify or explain why you have this desire for change. The angel already knows. Do not attempt to go into the details of what you want to change. The angel will work in a way that you cannot guess to bring your desired result.

You are talking to a spiritual being that is now in harmony with you, through the power of ritual. Although many people claim angels are too remote, too spiritual to understand our earthly needs, you will discover that they understand your needs and know solutions to them better than you can imagine. State your request plainly and with sincerity. This means you should say it briefly, clearly and with feeling. Feel your need as you say the words.

If we imagine that you are calling on Metatron to help you avoid looming bankruptcy, you do not need to tell the angel your excuses, your exact desires or who needs to do what, or how you think the problem would best be resolved. You need to ask for help. You do this by saying something as simple as, '…know that I ask to avoid bankruptcy, and return to financial stability.' If you mention a negative situation that you wish to avoid, it is wise to add in the positive outcome you actually seek, so rather than just saying you wish to avoid something, say what you want to achieve as well. You are avoiding bankruptcy, and seeking financial stability. That is as much detail as you need, and often it is quite simple. 'Know that I ask for my family to be at peace.' 'Know that I ask for this sickness to end and for health to return.'

The sincerity comes from how you feel when you say this. You are not begging the angel for help and you are not insisting on getting that help. Sincerity means that you feel, with all your heart, that this change is right for you. Sincerity means offering up that feeling of need, and believing that the angel will help. Although this part of the ritual is brief, so very, very brief, it is the core moment. Be sincere as you speak of your need, and know that the angel can help you.

You may be tempted to ask, beg, plead, explain or otherwise bargain with the angel, but this is not required and can lead to failed magick, as it goes against the essential nature of the process, which is your free will being asserted through the power of magick. A firm, clear, sincere statement of desire is all that's needed and expected. You will get to give thanks shortly, and that is all that's required for the circle of creation to be made complete.

Look at the sigil again, and know that Metatron (or whichever angel you are working with) remains present.

You will now say the words Ha-yah, Haw-yeh and Yee-yeh, while considering various thoughts and feelings. These words are derived from Hebrew terms, respectively meaning, 'was', 'is', and 'shall become'. You are stating your position in the flow of the universe. You acknowledge to the archangel that you have a past, that you exist in the present and that you have a strong desire for a future where things have changed from how they are now. This future arises directly out of your past and present.

Say Ha-yah three times (pronounced HAH-EE-AH), and as you say this, and in the moments that follow, think briefly about your problem. Think about when you became aware of it, how it grew, how it made you feel. If you finish saying the words and feel the need to linger on these thoughts and feelings, do so, but for no more than a minute. If you feel you've captured the feeling of the problem in the past, you can move on to the next word as soon as you say Ha-yah for the third time.

Say Haw-yeh three times (pronounced HAW-YEAH), and consider how you feel today, right now as you perform the ritual. You should be honest about your feelings. You may feel hopeful, even certain of change. You may still feel upset and bothered by the problem. Whatever your real feeling, and whatever negative thoughts and worries you have about the problem, let them come to you now as you say Haw-yeh three times. Do not linger in this state. When you have spoken the word for the third time, you may continue thinking about your current feelings for a few moments, but no more. Move to the next word.

Say Yee-yeh three times (pronounced YEE-YEAH), and feel absolute trust that what happens now is going to be absolutely the right thing. You surrender all thoughts of hope and know that whatever result the angel provides, in whatever form, at whatever time, is the most suitable result you could receive. This does not mean you'll get disappointing results, but that the result you get will be in harmony with where you are, the sincerity of your need and the ability of the angel. Your work, as you say this word three times, is to feel that whatever happens will be absolutely right.

You are not asking the angel to grant 'magick wishes', but to drive you to be all that you can be in the world. The angel will work wonders for you, but it is also expected that you will play your part, so you should offer to do so as you close the ritual. Say, 'I thank you Metatron, and promise that I will do all that I can to work with you in this endeavor.'

You are saying two things. Firstly, a sincere thanks that the angel is present and has heard you – it doesn't need to be more extensive than this. If you mean it when you say 'thank you' the angel knows, and you do not need to make offerings of any kind. Secondly, you are saying that you don't expect the angel to do all the work. If you want your liver to heal, you'll have to stop drinking alcohol. If you want to avoid that bankruptcy, you can't wait for it to happen – you need to do everything within your power to avoid it. Sometimes there is nothing you can do but trust and be patient. If that is all you can do, *do that*. There is always, always something you can do to attract the future you desire, and whatever it is, even if it's as simple as being patient and trusting, this you must do. Say these words to Metatron, or any angel you call, with sincerity. This is a promise you should keep. If you don't, no evil will befall you, but your magick will remain weak. When you fulfill that promise, the angels will move mountains to get you what you want. There should be no strain or struggle in your effort. Be calm, gentle, patient and assured, trusting the signs and omens that are given to you by the angels. Doing your part does not mean you have to do all the work. The angels will do most of it. In making any small effort, you signal that you genuinely want this reality, in your real life, not just during a ritual. That helps the angels to alter your universe.

You close the ritual by saying, 'Go in peace, Metatron.' This is not a command, but a polite way of saying that the ritual is over, and your needs have been met. Close your eyes for a moment, and when you open them, come back to normal reality, knowing that the ritual is over.

You only need to perform the ritual once, but you are welcome to perform it three or more times (though no more than once a day), if that helps you feel that you're getting everything to flow more effectively. There is no requirement to perform the ritual constantly for days on end. It is far more effective to stop and know that the magick is done, because that shows you *believe* the magick is working, which allows it to work.

You can perform your rituals on any day of the week and during any phase of the moon. If you prefer to time your magick to astrological phases you are welcome to, but it is not required for results.

You may have noted that in the above example, there was a call to Dynamis, which is unique to the archangel ritual. Other rituals contain words of power and Divine Names that are not shown here. All this will be clarified, where relevant, in each subsequent chapter.

To enable you to learn the pronunciation of the main Ritual Call, it is set out here phonetically:

In the Names of
ELL, ELL-OH-HEEM
ADD-OH-NIGH, ADD-EAR-EAR-ORN
EH-EE-EH ASHER EH-EE-EH
EL SHAD-EYE,
and by the Power of DYE-NAH-MISS,
I call on thee, _____.
I call thee, _____, by the power of
AH-KAH-TREE-ELL
EE-AH-OH-EH-TZAH-VAH-OAT
Hear my call, _____ and know
that I ask…

A small time spent learning these pronunciations will make it easy to adapt the ritual in the following chapters. All the pronunciation is available as a free audio-video guide at www.thepowerofmagick.com/angelic_pronunciations.html

That is all the instruction you need to be familiar with the ritual, and what follows in the rest of the book will detail one hundred and forty-two angels and archangels, along with their powers, and the relevant admitting words which ensure your call is heard. The instructions you need for making small adaptations to this ritual are provided where required.

In the time that follows the ritual you should remain open to intuition, to new ideas and if something feels like a solution, trust it. Look out for new people who may enter your life, or opportunities that come from unusual sources. Angels answer your requests in some many ways. Often, you don't notice that anything has happened until it is already long in the past.

If your problem remains after a few days, do not panic. Remain patient. If weeks go by, spend some time contemplating how you might ask in a different way, or what aspects of your life might need to change. It could be that you need to call on a different angel, to assist you with your own way of being, rather than external results. Magick can be a quick fix, a shortcut, a fast way to get something out of nowhere. Often it is a journey, so be willing to take that journey and make the small adjustments that lead to sudden breakthroughs.

When you do notice that your magick has worked, there is no need to call the angel. Often, you get an overwhelming feeling that you need to contact the angel. Know this – when you get that overwhelming feeling, the angel is with you in that very moment, and feels your gratitude. There is nothing more you need to do.

The Eight Angels of Virtue

There are eight Angels of Virtue, and they are named Symnay, Taftyah, Melech, Sezah, Safyn, Taftyarohel, Aeburatiel and Anyam. Their powers are described on the following pages, and these angels excel at bringing clarity, honesty and peace.

Whichever Angel of Virtue you call, the admitting words to be spoken are always the same. These words are: Soter, Volnah, Fabriel, Alesimus, pronounced as SOW-TER, VOLL-NAH, FAR-BREE-ELL and AL-ESS-EE-MUSS.

These words of power originate in various versions of *The Sixth and Seventh Books of Moses*. According to some authors, they are derived from names of God, but their exact origin is unclear. What is certain, however, is that words used to compel the compliance of angels are always considered sacred words of power, and are utterly free of evil.

A summary of the ritual process, along with the sigil, can be found in the following chapter.

These, then, are the Angels of Virtue and their powers:

The Angel Symnay

Symnay has the power to bring clarity in times of deception. If you are being deceived, Symnay will help you see the truth. Symnay is pronounced SIM-NEIGH.

The Angel Taftyah

Taftyah has the power to help you find peace in the middle of turmoil. When faced with great challenges, find endurance and strength through this angel. Taftyah is pronounced TAHF-TEE-AH.

The Angel Melech

Melech has the power to help you know the truth behind your desires. When you are obsessed with somebody or something, Melech can help you see if this is a desire of the soul, or a shallow distraction. Melech is pronounced MEL-ECK.

The Angel Sezah

Sezah has the power to bring answers in dreams. If you seek to know more about a situation or person, ask Sezah to bring the answer to you in a dream. Sezah is pronounced SEZ-AH.

The Angel Safyn

Safyn has the power to let others sense your honesty. If you feel mistrusted, by an individual or group, ask Safyn to let your honesty shine. Safyn is pronounced SAFF-EEN.

The Angel Taftyarohel

Taftyarohel has the power to help you meditate or rest. Ask the angel for help, and your long-term ability to relax and recuperate will improve. Taftyarohel is pronounced TAHF-TEE-AH-RAW-HEL.

The Angel Aeburatiel

Aeburatiel has the power to refresh you after illness or endurance. When you feel burdened by recovery or recent events, let this angel rejuvenate you. Aeburatiel is pronounced AY-BOOR-AH-TEA-ELL.

The Angel Anyam

Anyam has the power to clarify a relationship. If a friendship or relationship seems clouded, confusing or harmful, ask this angel to show you the true potential, and you will see if this person is good for you in the long-term. Anyam is pronounced AHN-YAHM.

Contacting The Angels of Virtue

The required sigil appears on the following page, and this same sigil is used for all eight Angels of Virtue. Insert the name of your chosen angel wherever you see _____.

Find a place to work your magick, and perform The Preparatory Ritual.

Look at the sigil and call the angel's name three times.

Make The Ritual Call as follows:

> In the Names of
> El, Elohim, Adonai, Adiriron
> Ehyeh-asher-Ehyeh, El Shadai,
> I call on thee, _____.
> Hear these words of power:
> Soter, Volnah, Fabriel, Alesimus
> I call thee, _____, by the power of
> Akatriel YHWH Tzvaot.
> Hear my call, _____ and know
> that I ask…

Speak your request.

Say the words Ha-yah, Haw-yeh and Yee-yeh, as instructed.

Thank the angel as instructed, and close the ritual by saying, 'Go in peace _____'.

The Sigil of The Angels of Virtue

The Nine Angels of Thrones

There are nine Angels of Thrones, and they are named Haseha, Amarzyom, Zawar, Yahel, Laheor, Adoyahel, Schimuel, Schaddyl and Parymel. Their powers are described on the following pages. The Angels of Thrones work primarily with emotions.

Whichever Angel of Thrones you call, the admitting words to be spoken are always the same. These words are: Tafa, Calphia, Calphas pronounced as TAH-FAH, CAL-FEE-AH and CAL-FASS.

Again, these words of power originate from *The Sixth and Seventh Books of Moses* and are sacred words of power, free of all evil.

A summary of the ritual process, along with the sigil, can be found in the following chapter.

These, then, are the Angels of Thrones and their powers:

The Angel Haseha

Haseha has the power to ease the heart of an enemy and bring forgiveness. Haseha is pronounced HAH-SEE-HAH.

The Angel Amarzyom

Amarzyom has the power to make your love known to another. If you have strong feelings for somebody, ask this angel to let the other person sense the depth of your love. Amarzyom is pronounced ARM-ARZ-EE-AWM.

The Angel Zawar

Zawar has the power to make others see you as agreeable, even though you may be forceful in your argument. An excellent angel to help you get your point across without offending others. Zawar is pronounced ZAH-WAH.

The Angel Yahel

Yahel has the power to make your family and loved ones appreciate you. If you feel unwanted or rejected, this will bring out the best in others, as they recall the feelings that have become hidden. Yahel is pronounced YAH-ELL.

The Angel Laheor

Laheor has the power to bring peace to a home that is filled with anger. Laheor is pronounced LAH-EE-AWE.

The Angel Adoyahel

Adoyahel has the power to help you forgive somebody who has wronged you. If you are trapped in your feelings, find the pathway to forgiveness here. Adoyahel is pronounced ADD-AWE-YAH-ELL.

The Angel Schimuel

Schimuel has the power to give you strength in a relationship that is suffering from external strain, or challenging life events. Shimuel is pronounced SHIM-OO-ELL.

The Angel Schaddyl

Schaddyl has the power to heal your heart when a relationship ends. Schaddyl is pronounced SHAD-EEL.

The Angel Parymel

Parymel has the power to give you courage when you are faced with a difficult, unknown or challenging situation that is expected to continue for some time. Parymel is pronounced PAR-EE-MEL.

Contacting The Angels of Thrones

The required sigil appears on the following page, and this same sigil is used for all nine Angels of Thrones. Insert the name of your chosen angel wherever you see _____.

Find a place to work your magick, and perform The Preparatory Ritual.

Look at the sigil and call the angel's name three times.

Make The Ritual Call as follows:

> In the Names of
> El, Elohim, Adonai, Adiriron
> Ehyeh-asher-Ehyeh, El Shadai,
> I call on thee, _____.
> Hear these words of power:
> Tafa, Calphia, Calphas
> I call thee, _____, by the power of
> Akatriel YHWH Tzvaot.
> Hear my call, _____ and know
> that I ask…

Speak your request.

Say the words Ha-yah, Haw-yeh and Yee-yeh, as instructed.

Thank the angel as instructed, and close the ritual by saying, 'Go in peace _____'.

The Sigil of The Angels of Thrones

The Archangels

There are twenty to thirty archangels, depending upon which sources you consult. While many people will be familiar with the angels Michael, Gabriel and Raphael (and some may also have heard of Uriel), there are many archangels that remain largely unknown. Most things in the occult are debated, but strangely enough, this isn't debated too often, because the term 'archangel' is not a definitive classification. It means something along the lines of 'great' or 'important' angel, and as such, many angels can belong to such a list. The eleven archangels in this book have been chosen because they are easy to contact and work with you in complete safety.

It is repeatedly argued that archangels should only be called on in dire circumstances, when all seems lost, and that they work only with major life changes. This is patently untrue, as there are many magickal methods that employ archangels to solve minor problems. Archangels can even be called easily enough that they are used to admit you into the presence of other 'lesser' angels. In this book, however, and using this method, it is absolutely vital that the angels are approached only when you are looking at long-term life changes, rather than smaller problems.

As you can see from the powers listed here, you are not trying to find a lost trinket or get a debt paid. These rituals work on the essence of who you are to become. Only invoke these angels if you seriously desire the change to occur. This is especially important because the angel's powers are described briefly. Metatron, for example, is said to answer sincere requests of any nature. It takes wisdom to know what to ask for, and when it is truly needed in your life. Don't call Metatron with this ritual and ask for instant fame and riches. Consider carefully, and ask with sincerity when you feel that it is right to ask for this particular kind of assistance.

Archangels are also fabled to work slowly, but again, nothing could be further from the truth. You may detect instant change, but you should also be patient enough to allow changes to occur gradually. The speed of change depends on many factors that are beyond your knowledge, so it is the last thing you should concern yourself with.

The main Ritual Call includes the key phrase, 'and by the Power of Dynamis', which is not found in the other ritual calls. Dynamis is not an angel or spirit, but is the embodiment of power. It is a Greek term, often used in magick, popularized by gnostic magicians. It remains an effective word for calling on the active form of the power of God within the material world. It is a way of asking for the power of God to work in the world. This is of particular note because it is one of those words that is poorly explored online, and could cause some confusion. When calling on archangels, this word - this power - is a very effective way to make sure the angel knows that you are asking for results that you can feel and know in the real world, rather than simply for knowledge or understanding.

The pronunciations given for the archangels are based on workings of the original Hebrew. You might know of the archangel Michael already, and in your mind the name is said just like the name Michael. You are free to use a modern pronunciation if that works for you. The pronunciations given here work well, but you can always use your own.

The Archangel Metatron

Pronounced as: MET-AH-TRAWN

Aids those striving for personal perfection.
Answers sincere requests of any nature.
Enables you to think deeply about matters of import.

The Archangel Raziel

Pronounced as: RAH-ZEE-ELL

Brings answers when you need them most.
Helps you to develop ideas.
Helps you to understand magick and manifestation.

The Archangel Tzaphqiel

Pronounced as: TSAFF-KEY-ELL

Enables clear communication when speaking.
Gives power to the written word.

The Archangel Zadkiel

Pronounced as: ZAHD-KEY-ELL

Gives you the power to improve memory, and recall knowledge easily.
Promotes release from oppression.

The Archangel Michael

Pronounced as: MEEK-AH-ELL

Gives you courage.
Helps you find a new direction or purpose.
Helps you see a task through to completion.

The Archangel Haniel

Pronounced as: HAH-KNEE-ELL

Encourages feelings of love to flourish.
Enables you to bring change to a situation that appears frozen.
Restores passion to a relationship that has become jaded.

The Archangel Raphael

Pronounced as: RAH-FAH-ELL

Brings healing to yourself, or to other people that you name.
Brings relief from all kinds of suffering.

The Archangel Gabriel

Pronounced as: GAH-BREE-ELL

Helps in your quest to seek redemption for actions you regret.
Assists you in making wise decisions in times of crisis.
Furthers your quest to know yourself.

The Archangel Sandalphon

Pronounced as: SAHN-DAHL-FAWN

Offers protection from evil, whether human or supernatural.
Gives you clarity on any issue of personal import.

The Archangel Uriel

Pronounced as: AWE-REE-ELL

Helps you to find practical solutions to problems.
Enables you to find spiritual answers.

The Archangel Jophiel

Pronounced as: EE-OH-FEE-ELL

Gives inspiration to artists and improves all artistic work.
Brings beauty to any endeavor.

The Archangel Ritual

The angelic sigils appear on the following pages, one to each page. If you are confident enough to learn the ritual word for word, you can, but it is perfectly acceptable to write out a summary of the ritual by hand, including your request as it will be spoken. This sheet of paper can be placed over any other sigil that may be visible (to cover it up), so your focus remains only on the sigil you want to work with. If using the eBook, only one sigil at a time will be shown, but the handwritten notes can be placed next to your device and used to guide the ritual.

Find a place to work your magick, and perform The Preparatory Ritual.

Look at the sigil and call the angel's name three times.

Make The Ritual Call as follows:

> In the Names of
> El, Elohim, Adonai, Adiriron
> Ehyeh-asher-Ehyeh, El Shadai,
> and by the Power of Dynamis,
> I call on thee, _____.
> I call thee, _____, by the power of
> Akatriel YHWH Tzvaot.
> Hear my call, _____ and know
> that I ask…

Speak your request.

Say the words Ha-yah, Haw-yeh and Yee-yeh, as instructed.

Thank the angel as instructed, and close the ritual by saying, 'Go in peace _____'.

The Sigil of Metatron

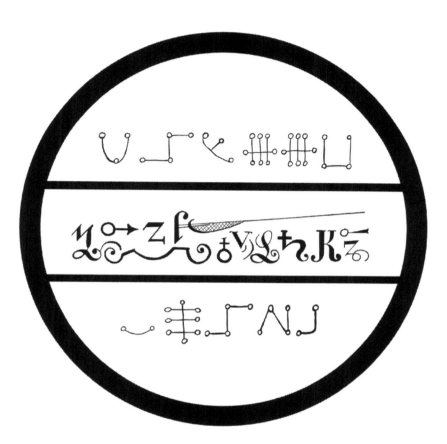

The Sigil of Raziel

The Sigil of Tzaphqiel

The Sigil of Zadkiel

The Sigil of Michael

The Sigil of Haniel

The Sigil of Raphael

The Sigil of Gabriel

The Sigil of Sandalphon

The Sigil of Uriel

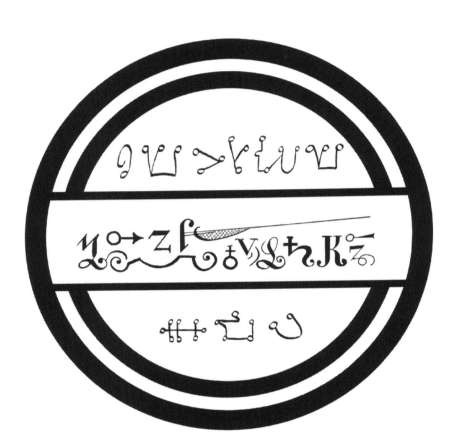

The Sigil of Jophiel

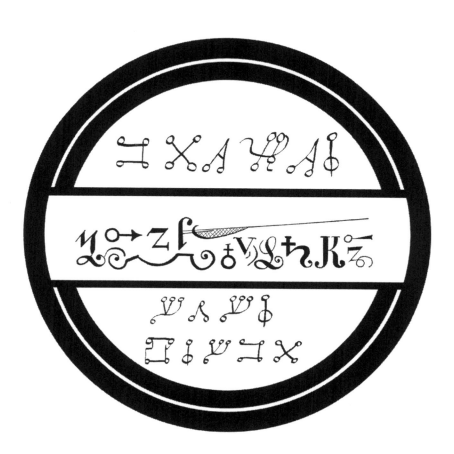

The Angels of The 72 Letter Name

The angels in this part of the book offer many ways to work on practical problems. The ritual structure for The 72 Angels is roughly the same as for other rituals, but you are given an Admitting Word that assists with the process. Each Admitting Word may appear to be nonsense. For the first angel, for example, this is the admitting word: EE-AH-HAH-VUH-HAH. This word combination is arrived at by combining divine names with the angelic name (in Hebrew), and this makes contact with the angel much more effective. It is, however, impossible to translate this admitting word, as it is effectively an anagram of the word God and the angel's name.

The angel names themselves have a fascinating origin, being based on The 72 Letter Name of God. There are many books written on the history and origin of The 72 Letter Name. You may be interested to know that three verses of Exodus (being 14: 19-21) are written right to left, with the next line going left to right, and the final line going right to left. In each resultant column, you find three letters, which gives you a sound. The first column gives you three letters that make the sound Vehu. Add the word El (meaning God), and you have Vehuel, which translates as The Angel Vehu of God. The first angel is Vehuel, and the other 72 angels are named in the same way.

Some authors do not use the El word ending, but instead choose iah, or 'Yah'. This is perfectly acceptable, but I have chosen to use El throughout, because I have found this consistency makes the magick effective. This means that you may find Vehuel being described as Vehuiah in other texts. This is of no concern unless you choose to be concerned about it. You can use either name and you will be contacting the same angel.

When researching these names you will find great inconsistency, especially online. For example, the twenty-fourth angel, in this book described as Chahoel (and pronounced as KAH-HAW-ELL) appears in many texts as Chahuiah or Hahuiah, and the last time I looked at Wikipedia the name was listed as Haniniah. As mentioned, there are many contradictions and variations, but you can be assured that what you find in this book is derived from interpretations of the original Hebrew, and these intonations have been found (over many years) to make for excellent contact with the correct angels. This is a source you can trust.

You should also take care to note that some angels, although quite distinct from one another, share similar names. Hahahel and Hahael are almost identical when written on the page, and even when spoken aloud, as are Daniel and Dahniel, but their sigils and powers are not at all the same. Be aware that they are, in fact, completely different angels.

You are also instructed to read out a line from a psalm as part of the ritual. If you research this subject, you will find that various sources suggest different psalms for each angel, other than those that are presented here. The lines from the psalms that I use have been found to be effective, possibly because each contains the angel's name embedded within the Hebrew text of the psalm. If you feel the need to use psalms from other traditions, you are welcome to explore.

Some authors would have you read the lines of the psalm in Hebrew, but I have found this is simply not necessary. You do not, after all, have to read the Bible in Hebrew to understand its meaning. Although Hebrew may be more authentic in some respects, English works perfectly well. Do note, however, that the psalm is only a key to the angel, and the psalm's meaning is often remote from the angel's assigned purpose. You speak the lines of the psalm only as part of the ritual process, and any apparent meaning does not contribute to what you are communicating to the angel.

As you are probably aware, there are countless versions of the Bible, and you are free to use your own if you have a favored translation of the psalms. You will note, however, that instead of God or Lord, the psalms in this book use the word Adonai (pronounced ADD-OH-NIGH). This wording is not essential, but has proven to be effective, and it is simply another name for God that is effective in magick.

If you study these angels, often known as the 'shem angels', or Angels of The Shemhamphoras, you will find many rules, regulations, and extensive dogma. Some authors insist that the only way to make contact is to draw the sigils by hand, in red ink, and circle them with Hebrew words. There are many other legends and rules, none of which apply here. The ritual can be performed just once, as with any ritual in this book.

While I admire some of the modern interpretations, I have found that you need nothing more than the angelic sigil, the angel's name, the chosen admitting word, and a sincere ritual process.

The sigils used here were obtained from a source that may not agree with everything you see or read elsewhere. I have found these to be the most elegant and effective sigils for these angels. In the case of the angel Kevekel, there are two sigils to choose from. The first is somewhat abstract, while the second appears to contain man-in-the-moon style faces. I have never been fond of that second version of the sigil, as it feels out of place, and is perhaps an error or an attempt to make something concrete from the abstract. Some occultists that I know well, however, disagree and find that it works more effectively for them. It felt right to include both versions, to give you the choice. If you work with Kevekel, choose the sigil that appeals to you.

The pronunciation of the admitting word and the angelic name should prove to be quite simple, but is also available online, on my website, if you need further guidance.

The angels have many powers, and they are described in brief, giving you enough information to ascertain whether or not the angel is suited to your problem. You do not need to call on several angels to solve a single problem. If you find, however, that there are several aspects to a problem, you can work with several angels at once to obtain your result. Wait a day between rituals, in such situations.

The 72 Angels Ritual

In each ritual, insert the angel's name wherever you see _____.

Find a place to work your magick, and perform The Preparatory Ritual.

Look at the sigil and call the angel's name three times.

Call the Admitting Word three times.

Read out the psalm for this ritual.

Make The Ritual Call as follows:

> In the Names of
> El, Elohim, Adonai, Adiriron
> Ehyeh-asher-Ehyeh, El Shadai,
> I call on thee, _____.
> I call thee, _____, by the power of
> Akatriel YHWH Tzvaot.
> Hear my call, _____ and know
> that I ask…

Speak your request.

Say the words Ha-yah, Haw-yeh and Yee-yeh, as instructed.

Thank the angel as instructed, and close the ritual by saying, 'Go in peace _____'.

The Angel Vehuel

The Admitting Word: EE-AH-HAH-VUH-HAH

The Call of Psalm 3:3 "But you, Adonai, are a shield around me, my glory, and the one who lifts up my head."

The Angel's Name: VEH-WHO-ELL

The Powers of Vehuel

Have a more open mind.
Understand science or mathematics.
Persuade clever people.
Improve your willpower.

The Angel Yeliel

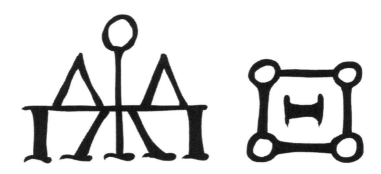

The Admitting Word: EE-EE-AH-LAH-VEE-AH

The Call of Psalm 22:19 "But don't be far off, Adonai. You are my help. Hurry to help me."

The Angel's Name: YELL-EE-ELL

The Powers of Yeliel

Find justice when you are opposed by family.
Find peace in a troubled relationship.

The Angel Sitel

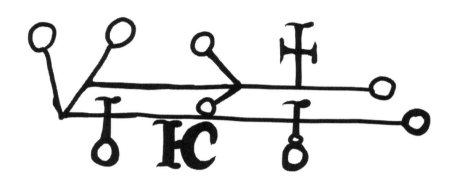

The Admitting Word: YEE-SAH-EE-VAH-TAH

The Call of Psalm 91:2 "I will say of Adonai, 'He is my refuge and my fortress; my God, in whom I trust.'"

The Angel's Name: SEAT-ELL

The Powers of Sitel

Protection against misfortune or calamity.
Communicate the truth.
Bring clarity to a relationship.

The Angel Elemel

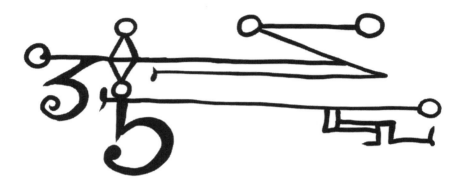

The Admitting Word: EE-AH-LAHV-MAH

The Call of Psalm 34:15 "The eyes of Adonai are toward the righteous. His ears listen to their cry."

The Angel's Name: ELL-EM-ELL

The Powers of Elemel

Ease spiritual torment.
Discover traitors.
Travel safely over long distances.
Discover new ways of working.

The Angel Mahashel

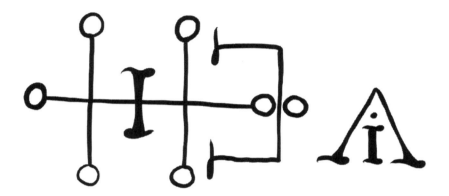

The Admitting Word: EEM-AH-HAHV-SHAH

The Call of Psalm 80:19 "Turn us again, Adonai, God of Armies. Cause your face to shine, and we will be saved."

The Angel's Name: MAH-HAH-SHELL

The Powers of Mahashel

Helps people to live in peace.
Stop others working magick.
Learn at great speed.

The Angel Lelahel

The Admitting Word: EE-LAH-LAH-VAH-HAH

The Call of Psalm 86:3 "Be merciful to me, Adonai, for I call to you all day long."

The Angel's Name: LEH-LAH-ELL

The Powers of Lelahel

Inspires new relationships and love.
Brings ease to sickness.
Helps you to acquire fame or reputation.

The Angel Achael

The Admitting Word: EE-AH-KEH-VAH

The Call of Psalm 3:5 "I laid myself down and slept. I awakened; for Adonai sustains me."

The Angel's Name: AK-AH-ELL

The Powers of Achael

Improves your ability to be patient.
Helps to promote a business venture.

The Angel Kahetel

The Admitting Word: EE-KAH-HAHV-TAH

The Call of Psalm 119:75 "Adonai, I know that your judgments are righteous, that in faithfulness you have afflicted me."

The Angel's Name: KAH-HET-ELL

The Powers of Kahetel

Protects against supernatural evil.
Helps the growth of food and crops.
Gives you a clear and powerful voice.

The Angel Heziel

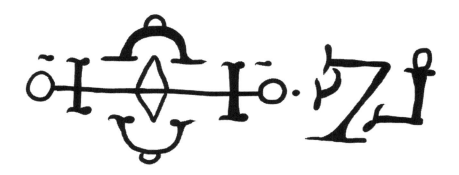

The Admitting Word: YAH-HEZ-VAY-AH

The Call of Psalm 88:14 "Adonai, why do you reject my soul? Why do you hide your face from me?"

The Angel's Name: HEZ-EE-ELL

The Powers of Heziel

Obtain the friendship of important people.
Urge somebody to keep a promise or pay a debt.
Encourage loyalty in those you work with.

The Angel Eladel

The Admitting Word: EE-AH-LAHV-DAH

The Call of Psalm 88:1 "Adonai, the God of my salvation, I have cried day and night before you."

The Angel's Name: ELL-ADD-ELL

The Powers of Eladel

Keep a secret from others.
Helps to heal disease.
Remove negative thoughts and habits.

The Angel Lavel

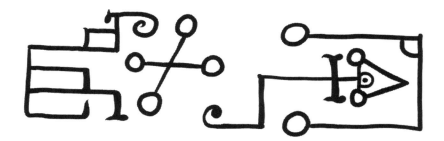

The Admitting Word: EE-LAH-AH-VAHV-AH

The Call of Psalm 27:13 "I am still confident of this: I will see the goodness of Adonai in the land of the living."

The Angel's Name: LAH-VELL

The Powers of Lavel

Let your abilities and talents become well known.
Influence those in power to show restraint.

The Angel Hahael

The Admitting Word: YAH-HAH-HAH-VAH

The Call of Psalm 6:4 "Return, Adonai. Deliver my soul, and save me for your loving kindness' sake."

The Angel's Name: HAH-HAH-ELL

The Powers of Hahael

Help others who are in great need of comfort.
Endure and overcome an adverse situation.
Convince wise people of your argument.

The Angel Yezelel

The Admitting Word: EE-YAH-ZAHV-LAH

The Call of Psalm 104:16 "Adonai's trees are well watered, the cedars of Lebanon, which he has planted;"

The Angel's Name: YEZ-ELL-ELL

The Powers of Yezelel

Reconcile lovers.
Improve friendship with one who remains aloof.
Obtain insight into the actions of those who influence you.
Learn new information and recall it easily.

The Angel Mebahel

The Admitting Word: EE-MAH-BAH-VAH-HAH

The Call of Psalm 9:9 "Adonai will also be a high tower for the oppressed; a high tower in times of trouble."

The Angel's Name: MEB-AH-ELL

The Powers of Mebahel

Protection from those who would take your money.
Make the truth become clear in a legal battle.
Make enemies reveal themselves through errors of judgement.

The Angel Hariel

The Admitting Word: EE-HAH-HAH-RAHV-EE-AH

The Call of Psalm 128:4 "Behold, thus is the man blessed who fears Adonai."

The Angel's Name: HAH-REE-ELL

The Powers of Hariel

Protect your emotions from negative people.
Discover new ways to create art.

The Angel Hakemel

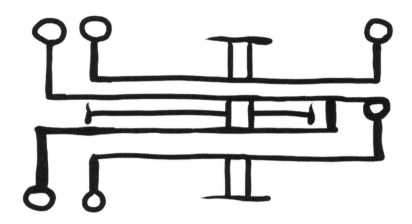

The Admitting Word: EE-AH-HAH-KAH-VAH-MAH

The Call of Psalm 10:1 "Why do you stand far off, Adonai? Why do you hide yourself in times of trouble?"

The Angel's Name: HAK-EM-ELL

The Powers of Hakemel

Prevent traitors from doing harm.
Obtain victory through clear and direct communication.

The Angel Lavahel

The Admitting Word: EE-LAH-AH-VAH-VAH

The Call of Psalm 105:1 "Give thanks to Adonai! Call on his name! Make his doings known among the peoples."

The Angel's Name: LAH-VAH-ELL

The Powers of Lavahel

Encourages peaceful sleep.
Eases sadness and depression.
Inspires musicians to create new work.

The Angel Keliel

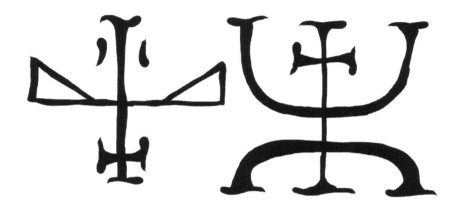

The Admitting Word: EE-KAH-LAH-VEE-AH

The Call of Psalm 103:21 "Praise Adonai, all you armies of his, you servants of his, who do his pleasure."

The Angel's Name: KELL-EE-ELL

The Powers of Keliel

Influence witnesses and dominate a legal trial.
Reveal your innocence in the face of accusation.
Cause enemies to be confused, and to lose interest in you.

The Angel Lovel

The Admitting Word: EE-LAH-VAH-VAH-VEH

The Call of Psalm 40:1 "I waited patiently for Adonai. He turned to me, and heard my cry."

The Angel's Name: LAW-VELL

The Powers of Lovel

Improve your level of intelligence and memory.
Become filled with charm and charisma.
Be well-liked by those who meet you.

The Angel Pahalel

The Admitting Word: EE-PAH-HAV-LAH

The Call of Psalm 119:108 "Accept, I beg you, the willing offerings of my mouth. Adonai, teach me your ordinances."

The Angel's Name: PAH-HAH-LELL

The Powers of Pahalel

Find a spiritual path through life.
Appreciate the wonder of creation in the moment.
Understand the needs that are the root cause of addiction.

The Angel Nelachel

The Admitting Word: EE-NAH-LAHV-KAH

The Call of Psalm 18:49 " Therefore I will give thanks to you, Adonai, among the nations, and will sing praises to your name."

The Angel's Name: NELL-AK-ELL

The Powers of Nelachel

Close the mouth of those who slander you.
Remove negative spirits from your home.
Understand mathematics more readily.

The Angel Yeyayel

The Admitting Word: EE-YAH-YAHV-YAH

The Call of Psalm 147:11 "Adonai takes pleasure in those who fear him, in those who hope in his loving kindness."

The Angel's Name: YEH-YAH-EE-ELL

The Powers of Yeyayel

Improves fortune in matters of business.
Makes business trips run smoothly.

The Angel Melahel

The Admitting Word: EE-MAH-LAH-VAH-HAH

The Call of Psalm 118:24 "This is the day that Adonai has made. We will rejoice and be glad in it!"

The Angel's Name: MEL-AH-ELL

The Powers of Melahel

Assists with safe travel over long distances.
Heals illness and injury.
Protects against injury from weapons.

The Angel Chahoel

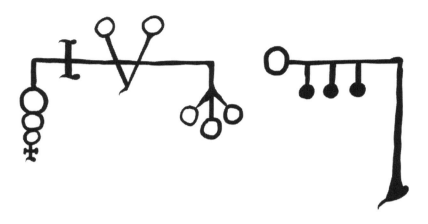

The Admitting Word: EE-KAH-HAH-VAH-VAH

The Call of Psalm 95:6 "Oh come, let's worship and bow down. Let's kneel before Adonai, our Maker, for he is our God."

The Angel's Name: KAH-HAW-ELL

The Powers of Chahoel

Protect your home or business from thieves.
Remove unwanted pests from your home.

The Angel Netahel

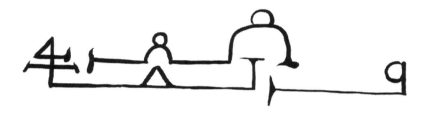

The Admitting Word: EE-NAH-TAHV-HAH

The Call of Psalm 34:4 "I sought Adonai, and he answered me, and delivered me from all my fears."

The Angel's Name: NET-AH-ELL

The Powers of Netahel

Find answers to your life's journey in your dreams.
Become wise regarding a subject of import.
Improve your ability to work with magick.

The Angel Haahel

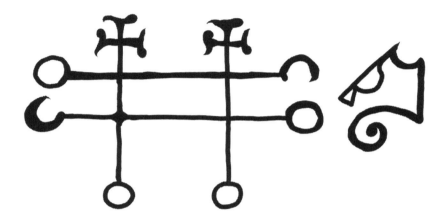

The Admitting Word: YAH-HAH-VAH

The Call of Psalm 97:1 "Adonai reigns! Let the earth rejoice! Let the multitude of islands be glad!"

The Angel's Name: HAH-AH-ELL

The Powers of Haahel

Protection from those who would discourage you.
Bring peace to a tumultuous relationship.
Communicate well with those who serve their own leaders.

The Angel Yeretel

The Admitting Word: EE-YAH-RAH-VAH-TAH

The Call of Psalm 140:1 "Deliver me, Adonai, from the evil man. Preserve me from the violent man."

The Angel's Name: YEAH-RET-ELL

The Powers of Yeretel

Make an enemy confused and unwilling to attack.
Bring peace to a conflicted workplace.

The Angel Shahahel

The Admitting Word: EE-SHAH-AH-VAH-AH

The Call of Psalm 35:24 "Vindicate me, Adonai my God, according to your righteousness. Don't let them gloat over me."

The Angel's Name: SHAH-AH-ELL

The Powers of Shahahel

Find practical solutions to complex problems.
Prevent disease from getting worse.
Maintain good health at an important time in your life.
Save a business or venture from collapse at times of crisis.

The Angel Riyiyel

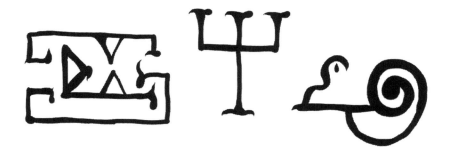

The Admitting Word: EE-RAH-YAHV-YAH

The Call of Psalm 9:11 "Sing praises to Adonai, who dwells in Zion, and declare among the people what he has done."

The Angel's Name: REE-YEE-YELL

The Powers of Riyiyel

Protect against hidden enemies.
Discover an enemy's identity when you feel you are under attack.
Discover secrets about those who affect your life.

The Angel Omael

The Admitting Word: YAH-HAV-VAH-MAH

The Call of Psalm 7:17 "I will give thanks to Adonai according to his righteousness, and will sing praise to the name of Adonai Most High."

The Angel's Name: AWE-MAH-ELL

The Powers of Omael

Relief when you feel desperate or frantic.
Improves patience in general.
To encourage fertility in men.

The Angel Lecavel

The Admitting Word: EE-LAH-KAHV-BAH

The Call of Psalm 31:14 "But I trust in you, Adonai. I said, "You are my God.""

The Angel's Name: LEK-AH-VELL

The Powers of Lecavel

Brings clarity and inspiration to your profession.
Helps you to remain inconspicuous.

The Angel Vesherel

The Admitting Word: EE-VAH-SHAHV-RAH

The Call of Psalm 116:4 "Then I called on Adonai's name: 'Adonai, I beg you, deliver my soul.'"

The Angel's Name: VESH-AIR-ELL

The Powers of Vesherel

Protects you from false accusations and restores reputation. Improves the quality of written projects.

The Angel Yichuel

The Admitting Word: EE-YAH-KAH-VAH-VEH

The Call of Psalm 92:5   "How great are your works, Adonai! Your thoughts are very deep."

The Angel's Name: YEE-KOO-ELL

The Powers of Yichuel

Make an enemies plans come undone.
Help those in authority see the truth.

The Angel Lehachel

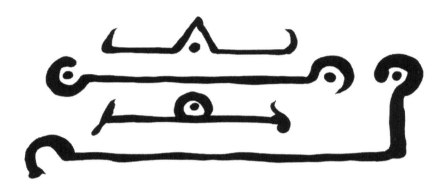

The Admitting Word: EE-LAHV-HAH-KAH

The Call of Psalm 98:4 "Make a joyful noise to Adonai, all the earth! Burst out and sing for joy, yes, sing praises!"

The Angel's Name: LEH-HACK-ELL

The Powers of Lehachel

Brings an end to anger between people or groups.
Inspires faithfulness.

The Angel Kevekel

The Admitting Word: EE-KAH-VAHV-KAH

The Call of Psalm 88:13 "But to you, Adonai, I have cried. In the morning, my prayer comes before you."

The Angel's Name: KEV-ECK-ELL

The Powers of Kevekel

Ensure a fair inheritance is obtained.
Heals damaged friendships and family feuds.

The Angel Kevekel – Version 2

This is an alternate version of the sigil, as explained in the main text. What follows is repeated from the previous page.

The Admitting Word: EE-KAH-VAHV-KAH

The Call of Psalm 88:13 "But to you, Adonai, I have cried. In the morning, my prayer comes before you."

The Angel's Name: KEV-ECK-ELL

The Powers of Kevekel

Ensure a fair inheritance is obtained.
Heals damaged friendships and family feuds.

The Angel Menadel

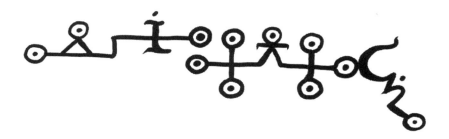

The Admitting Word: EE-MAH-NAH-VEH-DAH

The Call of Psalm 26:8 "Adonai, I love the habitation of your house, the place where your glory dwells."

The Angel's Name: MEN-AH-DELL

The Powers of Menadel

Helps reunite estranged family members.
Brings an end to gossip and slander.

The Angel Aniel

The Admitting Word: YAH-NAH-VAY-AH

The Call of Psalm 94:18 "When I said, 'My foot is slipping!'
Your loving kindness, Adonai, held me up."

The Angel's Name: AH-NEE-ELL

The Powers of Aniel

Assists with meditation.
Enables deep contemplation of important issues.
Encourages creative writing.

The Angel Chaamel

The Admitting Word: EE-KAH-HAH-VAH-MAH

The Call of Psalm 91:9: "Because you have made Adonai your refuge, and the Most High your dwelling place."

The Angel's Name: KAH-AH-MEL

The Powers of Chaamel

Repels against demonic curses.
Gives impetus to those who seek wisdom.
Endurance in the face of physical challenges.

The Angel Rehoel

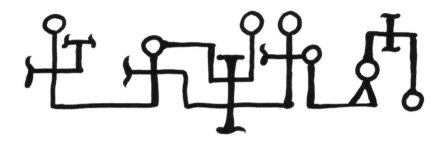

The Admitting Word: EE-RAH-HAH-VAH

The Call of Psalm 118:16 "The right hand of Adonai is exalted! The right hand of Adonai does valiantly!"

The Angel's Name: REH-HAW-ELL

The Powers of Rehoel

Recover when energy has been lost.
Ease the effects of an illness.
Improve your relationship with a parent.

The Angel Yeyizel

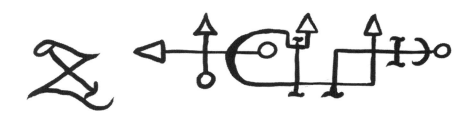

The Admitting Word: EE-YAH-EE-VAH-ZEH

The Call of Psalm 115:11 "You who fear Adonai, trust in Adonai! He is their help and their shield."

The Angel's Name: YEAH-EASE-ELL

The Powers of Yeyizel

Remove yourself from the attention of an enemy.
Improve artistic confidence and inspiration.

The Angel Hahahel

The Admitting Word: YAH-VAH-HEH-AH

The Call of Psalm 120:2 "Deliver my soul, Adonai, from lying lips, from a deceitful tongue."

The Angel's Name: HAH-HAH-AH-ELL

The Powers of Hahahel

Strengthens willpower.
Makes those who are unkind to you rethink their lives.

The Angel Michel

The Admitting Word: EE-MAH-YAHV-KAH

The Call of Psalm 121:7 "Adonai will keep you from all evil. He will keep your soul."

The Angel's Name: MEEK-ELL

The Powers of Michel

Influence those in positions of power.
Give power to a political cause to which you belong.

The Angel Vevalel

The Admitting Word: YEE-VAH-VAHV-LAH

The Call of Psalm 121:8 "Adonai will keep your going out and your coming in, from this time forward, and forever more."

The Angel's Name: VEH-VAH-LELL

The Powers of Vevalel

Improve general prosperity.
Be seen as a powerful and important person.

The Angel Yelahel

The Admitting Word: EE-YAH-LAH-VEH-HAH

The Call of Psalm 106:2 "Who can utter the mighty acts of Adonai, or fully declare all his praise?"

The Angel's Name: YELL-AH-ELL

The Powers of Yelahel

Be courageous when facing legal action.
Achieve victory in a legal battle.
Ease the mind in relations to difficult business concerns.

The Angel Sealel

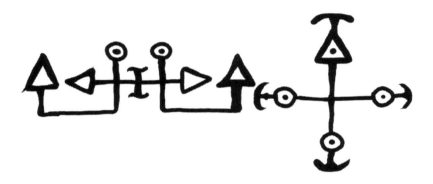

The Admitting Word: EE-SAH-HAH-VAH-LAH

The Call of Psalm 33:22 "Let your loving kindness be on us, Adonai, since we have hoped in you."

The Angel's Name: SEH-AH-LELL

The Powers of Sealel

Find a good teacher.
Rectify and unjust situation.

The Angel Ariel

The Admitting Word: EE-AH-RAHV-EE-AH

The Call of Psalm 38:21 "Don't forsake me, Adonai. My God, don't be far from me."

The Angel's Name: AH-REE-ELL

The Powers of Ariel

Discover new sources of income.
Find solutions to problems that appear overwhelming.
Experience more vivid dreams.

The Angel Eshalel

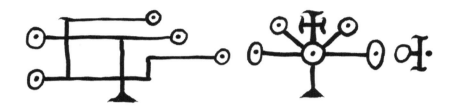

The Admitting Word: EE-AH-SHAH-VAH-LAH

The Call of Psalm 100:2 "Serve Adonai with gladness. Come before his presence with singing."

The Angel's Name: ESH-AH-LELL

The Powers of Eshalel

Contemplate the self and your true desires.
Understand where your future may take you.

The Angel Mihel

The Admitting Word: EE-MAH-EE-VAH-AH

The Call of Psalm 109:30 "I will give great thanks to Adonai with my mouth. Yes, I will praise him among the multitude."

The Angel's Name: MEE-HEL

The Powers of Mihel

Help a marriage remain loving.
Urges your spouse to support your dreams.

The Angel Vehuahel

The Admitting Word: EE-VAH-HAH-HAHV-AH

The Call of Psalm 145:3 "Great is Adonai, and greatly to be praised! His greatness is unsearchable."

The Angel's Name: VEH-WHO-AH-ELL

The Powers of Vehuahel

Bring peace where there is aggression.
Overcome the power of a great and influential personality.
Make those who are too proud become humble.

The Angel Daniel

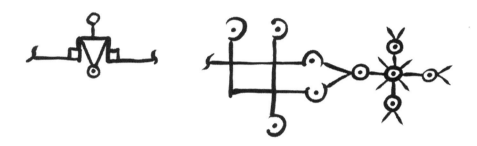

The Admitting Word: EE-DAH-NAHV-YAH

The Call of Psalm 9:1 "I will give thanks to Adonai with my whole heart. I will tell of all your marvelous works."

The Angel's Name: DAH-NEE-ELL

The Powers of Daniel

Helps recovery from grief.
Helps you to make inspired decisions on any issue.

The Angel Hachashel

The Admitting Word: EE-AH-HAH-KAHV-SHAH

The Call of Psalm 104:31 "Let Adonai's glory endure forever. Let Adonai rejoice in his works."

The Angel's Name: HAH-KAH-SHELL

The Powers of Hachashel

Helps you understand the workings of magick.
Enables you to hold many simultaneous thoughts during complex projects.
Improves clarity of thought under pressure.

The Angel Omemel

The Admitting Word: EE-AH-MAH-VEH-MAH

The Call of Psalm 25:6 "Adonai, remember your tender mercies and your loving kindness, for they are from old times."

The Angel's Name: AWE-MEM-ELL

The Powers of Omemel

Makes an enemy weak.
Helps you research effectively.
Brings vitality and enthusiasm to any activity.

The Angel Nenael

The Admitting Word: EE-NAH-NAHV-AH

The Call of Psalm 33:18 "Behold, Adonai's eye is on those who fear him, on those who hope in his loving kindness."

The Angel's Name: NEN-AH-ELL

The Powers of Nenael

Helps you to become an effective teacher.
Improves your skills in areas of science and craft.
Compels those who work in law to regard you well.

The Angel Nitel

The Admitting Word: EE-NAH-YAH-VAH-TAH

The Call of Psalm 16:5 "Adonai assigned my portion and my cup. You made my lot secure."

The Angel's Name: KNEE-TELL

The Powers of Nitel

Brings stability to families and organizations.
Gives your family or business a good reputation.

The Angel Mivahel

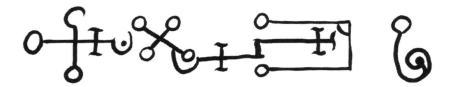

The Admitting Word: EE-MAH-BAH-VAH-AH

The Call of Psalm 103:19 "Adonai has established his throne in the heavens. His kingdom rules over all."

The Angel's Name: MEE-VAH-ELL

The Powers of Mivahel

Offers healing and love to others.
Encourages fertility.
Brings comfort and acceptance when genuine loss is unavoidable.

The Angel Pawiel

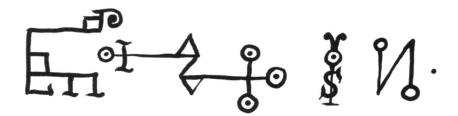

The Admitting Word: EE-PAH-VAHV-EE-AH

The Call of Psalm 149:4 "For Adonai takes pleasure in his people. He crowns the humble with salvation."

The Angel's Name: PAW-EE-ELL

The Powers of Pawiel

Bring what is asked for when a project nears completion.
Enables you to enjoy pleasure in moderation.
Brings fame and success to those who have long worked for it.

The Angel Nememel

The Admitting Word: EE-NAH-MAH-VAH-MAH

The Call of Psalm 145:14 "Adonai upholds all who fall, and raises up all those who are bowed down."

The Angel's Name: NEM-EM-ELL

The Powers of Nememel

Eases anxiety and fear that has no apparent source.
Helps those who work hard to prosper.

The Angel Yeyilel

The Admitting Word: EE-AH-LAHV-YAH

The Call of Psalm 113:2 "Blessed be Adonai's name, from this time forward and forever more."

The Angel's Name: YEAH-YEE-LELL

The Powers of Yeyilel

Heals emotional pain.
Enables you to let go of difficult memories.
Wards off those who are not enemies, but who are troublesome.

The Angel Harachel

The Admitting Word: EE-AH-HAH-RAHV-KAH

The Call of Psalm 94:22 "But Adonai has been my high tower, my God, the rock of my refuge."

The Angel's Name: HAH-RAH-KELL

The Powers of Harachel

Encourage female fertility and awareness of cycles.
Helps you control large amounts of money in business, without interference.

The Angel Metzerel

The Admitting Word: EE-MAHTS-VAH-RAH

The Call of Psalm 34:16 "Adonai's face is against those who do evil, to cut off their memory from the earth."

The Angel's Name: MET-ZAIR-ELL

The Powers of Metzerel

Heal your spirit after long endurance and suffering.
Make those who would bully you back off.

The Angel Umabel

The Admitting Word: EE-VAH-MAHV-BAH

The Call of Psalm 8:9 "Adonai, our Lord, how majestic is your name in all the earth!"

The Angel's Name: OO-MAH-BELL

The Powers of Umabel

Helps you obtain the genuine friendship of a specific person.
Enables love that fails to end in friendship.
Gives confidence to those who fear relationships.

The Angel Yahahel

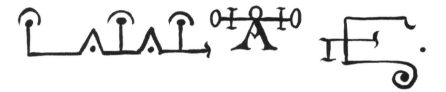

The Admitting Word: EE-AH-HAH-VAH-AH

The Call of Psalm 24:5 "He shall receive a blessing from Adonai, righteousness from the God of his salvation."

The Angel's Name: EE-AH-AH-ELL

The Powers of Yahahel

Helps you remain unseen when secrecy is required.
Helps secrets to be kept, even when others seek the truth.
Enables you to see wisdom in past failures.

The Angel Anuel

The Admitting Word: EE-AH-NAH-VAH-VEH

The Call of Psalm 37:4 "Also delight yourself in Adonai, and he will give you the desires of your heart."

The Angel's Name: AH-NOO-ELL

The Powers of Anuel

Bring protection to your business.
Helps you to make deals that serve your business well.
Avoid accidents in a risky work environment.

The Angel Machiel

The Admitting Word: EE-MAH-KAH-VAH-EE-AH

The Call of Psalm 30:10 "Hear, Lord, and have mercy on me.
Adonai, be my helper."

The Angel's Name: MAH-KEY-ELL

The Powers of Machiel

To bring skill to your written work.
Helps your words be well liked by the public.
Gives you the ability to promote yourself effectively.

The Angel Damebel

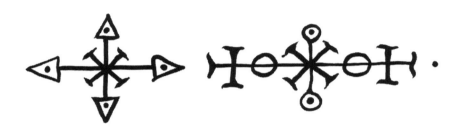

The Admitting Word: EE-DAH-MAH-VAH-BEH

The Call of Psalm 90:13 "Relent, Adonai. How long? Have compassion on your servants!"

The Angel's Name: DAM-EBB-ELL

The Powers of Damebel

Prevent evil sorcery from affecting your life.
Thrive in business.
Discover new ideas to expand your business.

The Angel Menakel

The Admitting Word: EE-MAH-NAHV-KAH

The Call of Psalm 87:2 "Adonai loves the gates of Zion more than all the dwellings of Jacob."

The Angel's Name: MEN-AH-KELL

The Powers of Menakel

Find peaceful sleep during difficult times.
Ease anger in one who is close to you.
Discover items that appear to be lost forever.

The Angel Iyahel

The Admitting Word: YAH-EE-VAH

The Call of Psalm 18:46 "Adonai lives! Blessed be my rock. Exalted be the God of my salvation."

The Angel's Name: EE-YAH-ELL

The Powers of Iyahel

Discover a breakthrough when all seems lost.
Discover strength in adversity.
Encourage change to move your life forward.

The Angel Chavuel

The Admitting Word: EE-KAH-BAH-VAHV-AH

The Call of Psalm 132:13 "For Adonai has chosen Zion. He has desired it for his habitation."

The Angel's Name: KAH-VOO-ELL

The Powers of Chavuel

Speed recovery when a disease wanes.
Strengthen yourself before an undertaking.

The Angel Raahel

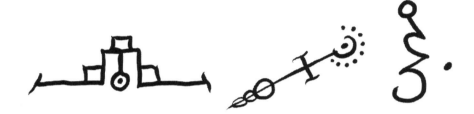

The Admitting Word: EE-RAH-AH-VAH-AH

The Call of Psalm 119:145 "I have called with my whole heart. Answer me, Adonai! I will keep your statutes."

The Angel's Name: RAH-AH-ELL

The Powers of Raahel

Increase fame or reputation.
Find possessions that have been stolen.

The Angel Yabamel

The Admitting Word: EE-YAH-BAH-VAH-MAH

The Call of Psalm 145:17 "Adonai is righteous in all his ways, and gracious in all his works."

The Angel's Name: YAH-BAH-MEL

The Powers of Yabamel

Brings harmony and calm.
Helps you regenerate and heal after turmoil.

The Angel Hayiel

The Admitting Word: YAH-AH-YAH-VAH-YAH-AH

The Call of Psalm 121:5 "Adonai is your keeper. Adonai is your shade on your right hand."

The Angel's Name: HAH-YEE-ELL

The Powers of Hayiel

Returns curses malice and cruelty to those who dispense them. Encourages bravery in the face of difficult odds.

The Angel Mumiel

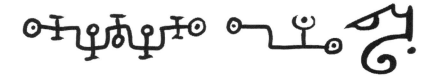

The Admitting Word: YAH-MAH-VEH-VAH-MAH

The Call of Psalm 131:3 "Israel, hope in Adonai, from this time forward and forever more."

The Angel's Name: MOOM-EE-ELL

The Powers of Mumiel

Brings a venture to a happy conclusion.
Helps you reap the full benefits of your medical treatment.

The Angels of The 42 Letter Name

The 42 Angels are neglected from magickal practice, being concerned with self-discovery, personal power and intuition. By grounding yourself in spiritual magick, you make the most progress through life. I strongly counsel you to work with these angels, even though they appear less glamorous.

The angel names originate from The 42 Letter Name of God. This Name itself is shrouded in mystery. Although it is encoded in the famous Ana Bekoach prayer, its origins are more ancient, being found in texts such as *Sefer Raziel*. Take the first letter of The 42 Letter Name and you get the first letter of Orpaniel, the first angel in the list. Take the second letter, and it gives you the first letter of Boel, the second angel. This continues, with each letter from the Name giving you the first letter of an angelic name, right through to Tavriel, the forty-second angel. Each name ends in El, meaning the angel is 'of God'. The complete etymology remains a subject of debate, but we are clear on the origin of the first letter and the El ending.

The Opening Key Word is derived from a combination of letters from The 42 Letter Name, while the Admitting Word is found in various ancient texts that list Divine Names that accompany each angelic name. If you notice that KUH-RAH-SUH-TAHN, ends in a word that almost sounds like Satan, don't be alarmed! KUH-RAH-SUH-TAHN is actually used in Kabbalah to fend off evil. If translated directly it means 'remove evil', and so is a very safe and holy part of this working.

It is unquestionable that more elegant sigils exist for these angels. In Damon Brand's *The Angels of Alchemy*, the angelic names are written in Hebrew, with words circling each sigil. I cannot fault a striking visual approach, but although more basic, the sigils in this book have worked for many. The angelic names are written in a rudimentary form of Phoenician. When you combine this sigil-word with an Opening Key Word and an Admitting Word, you contact the angel immediately.

The 42 Angels Ritual

In each ritual, insert the angel's name wherever you see _____.

Find a place to work your magick, and perform The Preparatory Ritual.

Say the Opening Key Word three times.

Look at the sigil and call the angel's name three times.

Say the Admitting Word three times.

Make The Ritual Call as follows:

> In the Names of
> El, Elohim, Adonai, Adiriron
> Ehyeh-asher-Ehyeh, El Shadai,
> I call on thee, _____.
> I call thee, _____, by the power of
> Akatriel YHWH Tzvaot.
> Hear my call, _____ and know
> that I ask…

Speak your request.

Say the words Ha-yah, Haw-yeh and Yee-yeh, as instructed.

Thank the angel as instructed, and close the ritual by saying, 'Go in peace _____'.

The Angel Orpaniel

Opening Key Word: AHV-GEE-TAHTZ

Admitting Word: AH-DEER-EAR-ORN

The Angel's Name: ORP-AH-NEE-ELL

The Powers of Orpaniel

Healing emotional pain.
Open your heart to God.

The Angel Boel

∠𝕂Y∃

Opening Key Word: AHV-GEE-TAHTZ

Admitting Word: BAH-HEAR-YAH-AWN

The Angel's Name: BOW-AH-ELL

The Powers of Boel

Inner strength.
Honesty in adversity.

The Angel Gavriel

Opening Key Word: AHV-GEE-TAHTZ

Admitting Word: GUH-VEER-EE-AH-RAWN

The Angel's Name: GAH-VREE-ELL

The Powers of Gavriel

Discover your purpose.
Feel inner strength.
Understand family.

The Angel Iophiel

Opening Key Word: AHV-GEE-TAHTZ

Admitting Word: YEEG-BAH-HE-AH

The Angel's Name: EE-OH-FEE-ELL

Note: This is pronounced in the same way as the archangel Jophiel, but is a different angel entirely.

The Powers of Iophiel

Become inspired to create art.
Develop creatively through intense work.
Improve your perception.

The Angel Tumiel

Opening Key Word: AHV-GEE-TAHTZ

Admitting Word: TEH-LAH-ME-AH

The Angel's Name: TOO-ME-ELL

The Powers of Tumiel

Let go of guilt.
Remember true feelings for a loved one.

The Angel Tzadkiel

Opening Key Word: AHV-GEE-TAHTZ

Admitting Word: TSUT-AHN-EE-AH

The Angel's Name: TSAD-KEY-ELL

The Powers of Tzadkiel

Be seen as a leader.
Develop leadership skills and confidence.
Make your voice such that others heed you when you speak.

The Angel Kavtziel

Opening Key Word: KUH-RAH-SUH-TAHN

Admitting Word: KUH-RAHM-EE-AH

The Angel's Name: KAHV-TSEE-ELL

The Powers of Kavtziel

Feel relaxed in situations that arouse anxiety.
Master the art of easy conversation.

The Angel Ravchiel

Opening Key Word: KUH-RAH-SUH-TAHN

Admitting Word: RUH-GAH-REE-AH

The Angel's Name: RAHV-KEY-ELL

The Powers of Ravchiel

Rediscover your passion for life.
Rejuvenate a relationship.

The Angel Oziel

Opening Key Word: KUH-RAH-SUH-TAHN

Admitting Word: EE-REE-REE-AH

The Angel's Name: AWE-ZEE-ELL

The Powers of Oziel

Break habits and addiction.
Find the courage to change.
Willpower to overcome habits or addictions.

The Angel Shemshiel

Opening Key Word: KUH-RAH-SUH-TAHN

Admitting Word: SHUH-GAH-EE-AH

The Angel's Name: SHEM-SHE-ELL

The Powers of Shemshiel

Insight into blockages in your life.
Understand who may be holding back your potential.

The Angel Tofiel

Opening Key Word: KUH-RAH-SUH-TAHN

Admitting Word: TEH-LAH-TEE-AH

The Angel's Name: TORE-FEE-ELL

The Powers of Tofiel

Find peace when a situation makes you afraid.
Ease fear of the unknown or dark expectations.

The Angel Nagriel

Opening Key Word: KUH-RAH-SUH-TAHN

Admitting Word: NUH-HAH-DEE-AH

The Angel's Name: NAHG-REE-ELL

The Powers of Nagriel

Achieve greatness in marketing or spreading a message.
Gives potency to speeches and presentations.

The Angel Nachliel

Opening Key Word: NAH-GAH-DEE-KESH

Admitting Word: KNEE-SHMAH-REE-AH

The Angel's Name: NAK-LEE-ELL

The Powers of Nachliel

Ease emotional suffering.
Overcome the loss of a friend.

The Angel Gavoriel

Opening Key Word: NAH-GAH-DEE-KESH

Admitting Word: GAH-REE-AH

The Angel's Name: GAH-VORE-EE-ELL

The Powers of Gavoriel

Find harmony in times of distress.
Be peaceful when those around you are losing control.
Bring calm to relationships that are restless or uneasy.

The Angel Dahniel

Opening Key Word: NAH-GAH-DEE-KESH

Admitting Word: DAH-REE-AH

The Angel's Name: DAH-NEE-ELL

The Powers of Dahniel

Discover imbalance and see how it can be restored to balance.
Gain insight into aspects of your life that are damaging.
When you feel drained, discover what takes your energy.

The Angel Yehodiel

Opening Key Word: NAH-GAH-DEE-KESH

Admitting Word: YAH-LEE-AH

The Angel's Name: YEAH-HOARD-EE-ELL

The Powers of Yehodiel

Know the true depth and potential of a fledgling relationship. See beyond surface emotions to know how you really feel.

The Angel Kevashiel

Opening Key Word: NAH-GAH-DEE-KESH

Admitting Word: KAH-SEE-AH

The Angel's Name: KEV-AH-SHE-ELL

The Powers of Kevashiel

Overcome destructive obsessions.
Find release from feelings of desperation.
Let an overwhelming problem move to the back of your mind.

The Angel Shahariel

∠ K ⊒ ⊣ O W

Opening Key Word: NAH-GAH-DEE-KESH

Admitting Word: SHEEG-YORN-YAH

The Angel's Name: SHAH-HAH-REE-ELL

The Powers of Shahariel

Remove spite that occurs due to habit.
Recover the spark of love that initiated your relationship.

The Angel Berachiel

Opening Key Word: BAH-TRAHTS-TAHG

Admitting Word: BAW-AHL-EE-AH

The Angel's Name: BEH-RAH-KEY-ELL

The Powers of Berachiel

Provides intuition regarding a specific situation.
Improves intuition and trust.
Increases synchronicity, omens and signs.

The Angel Tahftiel

Opening Key Word: BAH-TRAHTS-TAHG

Admitting Word: TORE-AH-REE-AH

The Angel's Name: TAHF-TEE-ELL

The Powers of Taftiel

Gain insights into new ideas and their potential.
Understand what is going on behind a problem.

The Angel Rachmiel

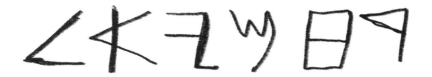

Opening Key Word: BAH-TRAHTS-TAHG

Admitting Word: RAHM-YAH

The Angel's Name: RACK-ME-ELL

The Powers of Rachmiel

Recover a sense of wonder.
Feel renewed and cleansed of your mistakes.

The Angel Tzafuniel

Opening Key Word: BAH-TRAHTS-TAHG

Admitting Word: TSAH-TSAH-TSEE-YAH

The Angel's Name: TSAH-FOO-NEE-ELL

The Powers of Tzafuniel

Keep faith in yourself when the odds are against you.
Patience and strength when faced with an ongoing challenge.

The Angel Trumiel

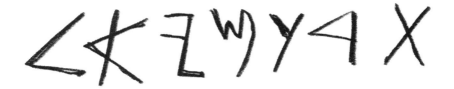

Opening Key Word: BAH-TRAHTS-TAHG

Admitting Word: TAH-HAH-VEE-HEE-YAH

The Angel's Name: TRUE-ME-ELL

The Powers of Trumiel

Let others see the good in you.
Find friendship when travelling or when moving to a new area.

The Angel Gedodiel

Opening Key Word: BAH-TRAHTS-TAHG

Admitting Word: GAH-LAH-GAHL-EE-AH

The Angel's Name: GED-AWE-DEE-ELL

The Powers of Gedodiel

Remain unseen or unnoticed by an enemy.
Receive comfort from those you love.

The Angel Cheziel

Opening Key Word: KAH-KEV-ET-NAH

Admitting Word: KEEN-AHN-AH-YAH

The Angel's Name: KEZ-EE-ELL

The Powers of Cheziel

Attract prophetic dreams.
Learn to visualize with clarity.

The Angel Kumiel

Opening Key Word: KAH-KEV-ET-NAH

Admitting Word: KAH-TAH-KAH-YAH

The Angel's Name: KOO-ME-ELL

The Powers of Kumiel

Recover from mental stress.
Renew your spirit when overworked.

The Angel Barkiel

Opening Key Word: KAH-KEV-ET-NAH

Admitting Word: BEH-HAHV-HAHV-EE-AH

The Angel's Name: BARK-EE-ELL

The Powers of Barkiel

Clear thought when originating ideas.
Remain focussed during exams and other mental challenges.
Communicate clearly to an individual when your message is
not getting through.

The Angel Tahariel

Opening Key Word: KAH-KEV-ET-NAH

Admitting Word: TAH-VEH-HAW-YAH

The Angel's Name: TAH-HAH-REE-ELL

The Powers of Tahariel

Break a cycle or habit of negative thought.
See a person clearly, without negative preconceptions.
Become at peace on a long journey.

The Angel Nuriel

⌐K⌐⊣Y⅄

Opening Key Word: KAH-KEV-ET-NAH

Admitting Word: NUH-TAH-NEE-AH

The Angel's Name: NOO-REE-ELL

The Powers of Nuriel

Improve self-confidence, especially in the face of excessive criticism.
Courage when performing or speaking in public.

The Angel Amiel

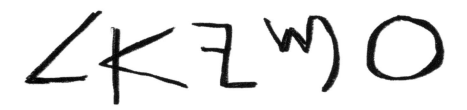

Opening Key Word: KAH-KEV-ET-NAH

Admitting Word: AH-MAH-MAH-YAH

The Angel's Name: AH-ME-ELL

The Powers of Amiel

Project charisma and let your attractive qualities shine.
Feel relaxed in social situations.

The Angel Yisrael

Opening Key Word: YAHG-LEFF-ZAWK

Admitting Word: YEH-HAHL-SHUH-RAH-YAH

The Angel's Name: YEES-RAH-ELL

The Powers of Yisrael

Find truth and inspiration in daydreams.
Let creative thought become free and imaginative.
Improve a work of art through active imagination.

The Angel Gahdiel

Opening Key Word: YAHG-LEFF-ZAWK

Admitting Word: GORE-EAR-AH-EE-AH

The Angel's Name: GAH-DEE-ELL

The Powers of Gahdiel

Define clear intentions.
Find the willpower to commit to long-term projects.
Remove obstacles from your true path in life.

The Angel Lahaviel

Opening Key Word: YAHG-LEFF-ZAWK

Admitting Word: LEH-ME-MAH-REE-AH

The Angel's Name: LAH-HAH-VEE-ELL

The Powers of Lahaviel

Find clarity when emotions are unclear.
See beyond the deceit of others.
Know whether or not you can trust a promise.

The Angel Pahniel

Opening Key Word: YAHG-LEFF-ZAWK

Admitting Word: PEH-CORE-KAH-REE-AH

The Angel's Name: PAH-NEE-ELL

The Powers of Pahniel

Be noticed and stand out in a crowd.
Project warmth and love to an individual, through all your words and actions.

The Angel Zachriel

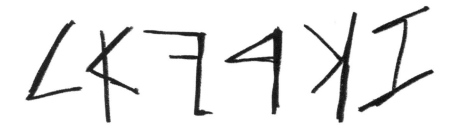

Opening Key Word: YAHG-LEFF-ZAWK

Admitting Word: ZUH-HAH-RUH-ZAH-HAH-REE-AH

The Angel's Name: ZAK-REE-ELL

The Powers of Zachriel

Attract coincidence and change that leads to growth.
Let new ideas lead you to a new life.

The Angel Kedoshiel

Opening Key Word: YAHG-LEFF-ZAWK

Admitting Word: KEH-MAH-LEE-YAH

The Angel's Name: KED-AWE-SHE-ELL

The Powers of Kedoshiel

Stay true to your plans when others would dissuade you.
Project firm authority to those who defy or question you.

The Angel Shelgiel

Opening Key Word: SHAH-COOTS-EAT

Admitting Word: SHAH-TEH-HOARD-RAH-YAH

The Angel's Name: SHELL-GEE-ELL

The Power of Shelgiel

Overcome confusion and despair, to see a way forward.

The Angel Karviel

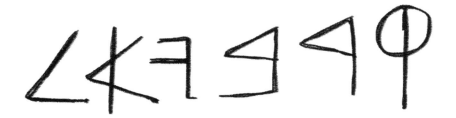

Opening Key Word: SHAH-COOTS-EAT

Admitting Word: KAH-DAW-SHE-AH

The Angel's Name: KAH-VEE-ELL

The Power of Karviel

Bring the end of a situation more rapidly.
Get more done in a short length of time.

The Angel Vaviel

Opening Key Word: SHAH-COOTS-EAT

Admitting Word: VEH-HAH-AH-LAYL-EE-AH

The Angel's Name: VAH-VEE-ELL

The Power of Vaviel

Let your beauty and truth be seen by another, or by a group of people.
Discover true feelings that lie beyond infatuation.

The Angel Tzuriel

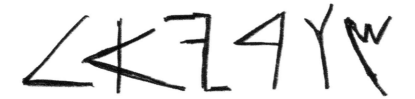

Opening Key Word: SHAH-COOTS-EAT

Admitting Word: TSAH-DEE-YAH

The Angel's Name: TSOO-REE-ELL

The Power of Tzuriel

Attract random moments of fortune in times of difficulty.
Attract opportunities for pleasure, discovery and travel.

The Angel Ialpiel

Opening Key Word: SHAH-COOTS-EAT

Admitting Word: YEET-HAH-REH-REE-AH

The Angel's Name: EE-AL-PEA-ELL

The Power of Ialpiel

Remove weariness and feel able to continue.
Discover what you can leave behind.
Move on from people who weigh you down.

The Angel Tavriel

Opening Key Word: SHAH-COOTS-EAT

Admitting Word: TAHM-TAIL-EE-AH

The Angel's Name: TAHV-REE-ELL

The Power of Tavriel

Improve your ability to persist with a project or venture that matters to you.
Gain insight to the true value of what you are working on.

The Meaning of Names

It can be discomforting to call out strange sounds without knowing what they mean, so I have attempted to explain them briefly but clearly.

El, Elohim and Adonai are Biblical names of God.

Adiriron has its root in a Hebrew word for might or strength, and is regarded as a Divine name in kabbalah.

Ehyeh-asher-Ehyeh is given as a name of God, but also translates in many ways approximating to, 'I will be what I will be'.

El Shadai is a name of God, more specifically translated as 'God Almighty'.

Akatriel is a Divine Name from kabbalah, related to manifestation.

YHWH Tzvaot is a name that contains the Tetragrammaton (YHWH), followed by the word Tzvaot. It is translated in many ways, but is used here as God of Hosts, meaning a form of power in the world.

Ha-yah means 'was'. Haw-yeh means 'is'. Yee-yeh means 'shall become'.

The other words are explored, where relevant, within the main text.

Find Out More

In all that has gone before in this book, I am relying on you to interpret much of the information, because this interpretation is a part of the process you undergo with magick. The angelic powers are described in brief, not to confuse, but to give you the chance to reach out with your insight, to detect what may be right for you. If you see a power called, 'Overcome the loss of a friend,' does it mean you recover from grief after death, or that you get over a betrayal, or feel acceptance when a friend leaves town? This is up to you. When a power sounds like it *could* apply in many ways, it *does* apply in many ways. Remember this at all times, when choosing your angel.

I am unable to provide accurate references for all the work that has gone into this book, partly because I am not a professor, and in part because that's the nature of occultism. What's missing from any list of books are the secret materials, the occult works that make true sense of the magick. This practical magick is passed through secret societies, occult organizations and the like. Some of it is shared in this book, and hopefully in other books to follow.

Thank you for taking the time to read this book. I hope you are able to enjoy the benefits of magick by entering into the rituals with an open heart and an open mind. If you can do that, I trust that you will be duly rewarded.

Ben Woodcroft

How Magick is Shared

Thank you for buying this book from The Power of Magick Publishing. We are a small, enthusiastic company and we greatly appreciate your purchase. We hope to keep publishing occult books, but there is something we should share with you.

For almost a century, publishing was a difficult and expensive business. Everything changed with Amazon. Suddenly, anybody could publish a book, free. Those glory years were short-lived. It's all changed again.

Anybody *can* still publish a book on Amazon, but unless you spend a lot of money, your book will vanish into obscurity. You now have to pay a lot of money to make sure your book is seen in the right place on Amazon product pages.

Many people believe publishing is an easy way to make money, but a book like this costs us several thousand dollars before it even goes on sale. We have to pay a small advance to the author, and we pay our editor, a copy editor, a cover designer, a proofreader, and then invest in marketing – without that, no book could last more than a week.

Amazon and other distributors, charge for printing and digital distribution of every single copy. The actual profit we make on each book sold is only a few cents. Making a book pay for itself is extremely difficult.

Publishing is now a very challenging business, and occult books sell in small quantities. We accept that challenge because we have a lot that we want to share. You can help. If you enjoyed the book, please write a review on Amazon.com or Goodreads, so that people know we are doing something worthwhile.

We hope our small company can continue to bring you the books you care about. Thank you.

Chris Wood
The Power of Magick Publishing

www.thepowerofmagick.com

Made in the USA
Middletown, DE
30 May 2023

31774152R00104